THE

Vegan Dairy
COOKBOOK

Make Your Own
Plant-Based Mylks, Cheezes,
and Kitchen Staples

MARLEEN VISSER

TRANSLATED BY NINA WOODSON

Skyhorse Publishing

CONTENTS

PREFACE

When I realized recently that the plant-based frozen yogurt I was eating was made from homemade yogurt that itself was made from homemade soy milk in which only organic soybeans had been used, I became even more excited about writing this book full of vegan dairy basics and uses for them.

Although I did not originally set out to make a "from scratch" cookbook of vegan dairy recipes, that is what ended up occurring naturally. It is in my nature to make food starting with basic ingredients. I like the idea of clean eating, and homemade products are, of course, part of that. Plus, making your own plant-based dairy products is incredibly easy.

I started a few years ago by making nut milk and developing recipes to use the pulp that gets left over. Since then, I have created more and more vegan recipes using homemade dairy alternatives. One such item is vegan cheese, a product enjoying a surge in investment and rising quickly in popularity. But opinions on it remain divided, with strong views on either side. I personally think you need to be relatively open-cheese-minded when it comes to plant-based cheese and not compare it directly with traditional cheese. You need to see such cheeze—as I like to call it—more as a new variety with endless possible sub-varieties.

The vegan dairy products that more closely resemble what we are accustomed to are less controversial. Some of my favorites include: crème brûlée, chocolate mousse, béchamel sauce, ice cream (of every kind), yogurt, Dutch butter cake, lemon quark, vanilla pudding, chocolate pudding, tzatziki, mayonnaise, meringue, and more.

I greatly enjoyed working on this book: from developing the recipes and testing them endlessly in our tiny kitchen to the photography and the styling with Inge Pouw's magnificent props (The Secret Props Room). I hope you will be equally happy with it, whether you are fully vegan or just want to eat plant-based foods more often. Who knows? Maybe soon you too will be eating a popsicle made from your own homemade yogurt produced using mylk created in your own kitchen. In any event, enjoy!

If you have any questions, you can find me via my website marleenvisser.nl or on Instagram @marleenvisser. Please also share your creations on Instagram with #50xveganzuivel.

Marleen Visser

HOW TO USE THIS BOOK

This book consists of both recipes for basic vegan dairy ingredients and recipes in which you can use those ingredients. For the latter, I will always reference the basic ingredient recipe that is in the book, but you can also make the dishes using plant-based dairy products you buy at the store.

~~~~~~~

BASIC EQUIPMENT

The following items are handy to have for making the recipes in this book.

Food processor, blender, and immersion blender: For dense mixtures or mixtures that need to be mixed for a long time, such as nut mixtures, I generally use a food processor. When dealing with small quantities, a food chopper sometimes works better. For the more liquid mixtures, such as nut milk, I use a blender. And an immersion blender is ideal for things like mayonnaise.

Glass bottles and jars: For storing everything in, along with labels on which you can write the name of the item and the date it was made.

Measuring spoons: You will see a lot of the measurements in this book given in teaspoons and tablespoons. The measurements given assume that all ingredients are leveled off. For reference:

1 teaspoon = 5 mL and 1 tablespoon = 15 mL.

Silicone or porcelain molds: For making cheeze.

Strainer and cheesecloth: For the mylk recipes and some of the cheeze recipes. A nut milk bag (somewhat finer material) or hydrophilic cloth can often also be used.

Thermometer: For making yogurt.

STERILIZATION

Before storing your products in the refrigerator it is vital that you sterilize all the necessary tools.

You can do that as follows:

Wash glass bottles and jars thoroughly with soap and hot water, removing the lids and caps, then place them in a preheated oven set to 275°F (130°C). The lids and caps, which cannot be sterilized in the oven, can be placed in boiling water for a minimum of 10 minutes. This method also works for any other tools you want to sterilize. Place the glassware, lids and caps, and other tools on a clean tea towel and allow to dry and cool thoroughly.

You can sterilize cheesecloth by ironing it.

~~~~~~~~~~~~~~~~~~~~

BASIC INGREDIENTS

Apple cider vinegar: This is used in many of the savory recipes to add a bit more zest.

Aquafaba (chickpea liquid): It is ideal for making mayonnaise, whipped cream, and meringue.

Chickpea flour: This makes an excellent egg replacement. It is used in the recipes for French Toast and Scrambled Tofu (see on pages 33 and 129).

Coconut milk and coconut oil: Buy responsibly sourced coconut milk. There are still some brands of coconut milk that are not considered vegan because monkeys are used to harvest the coconuts. So, it is important to know which brands are cruelty-free and which are not. I use full-fat coconut milk and coconut oil that is unscented and refined.

Cream of tartar: You can use this as a stabilizer in such dishes as meringue.

Kala namak: The best vegan mayo I ever had was at a burger joint in Berlin. The owner revealed to me the secret ingredient that made it taste just like traditional mayonnaise: kala namak! This "black gold" from India is a volcanic rock salt that smells—strongly—of eggs and enhances overall flavor when it integrates into the dish. Besides the mayonnaise recipe, it is also used in the French toast and scrambled tofu recipes in this book.

Nutritional yeast: This has a cheesy flavor and is thus used in just about every cheeze recipe. It also makes a delicious salad topping.

Nuts: Nuts are an ideal base for vegan recipes, especially cashews because of their neutral flavor profile and soft texture. They are regularly used throughout this book.

Oils: I use a wide variety of oils, whereby I take into consideration the flavor profile (neutral is generally the best) and the smoke point, and thus applicability for any given recipe. Grapeseed oil is one that I have been using since I learned to make sauces at Le Cordon Bleu in Paris several years ago. It is perfect for making mayonnaise. Other useful oils are avocado oil, canola oil (but it must be organic and cold pressed), and mild olive oil.

Pink Himalayan salt: This is my favorite salt. You can substitute it for sea salt in any recipe that calls for that.

Psyllium husk: This helps make cheese stretchy. It is ideal for the Nozzarella and Cheeze Fondue (pages 114 and 122).

Tofu: I use regular (firm) tofu for the savory recipes and silken tofu for desserts.

~~~~~~~~~~~~~~~~~~~~~~~~~~~~~~

THICKENING AGENTS
There are a variety of thickening agents I use in this book. For custard-like substances (e.g., panna cotta and crème brûlée), I use agar-agar, and for puddings and sauces, I generally prefer organic cornstarch. Arrowroot is another thickener I often use, for example, together with agar-agar in yogurt.

Agar-agar: This is a pretty strong thickener, which means you only need the smallest amount. Slightly more or less of the powder can make a big difference, so be sure to weigh or measure it closely (1 teaspoon = 2 grams / 0.07 ounces). In addition, agar-agar—which is made from red algae—needs to be cooked for at least 2 minutes to work properly.

Arrowroot: You also need to be careful when using arrowroot. This is another strong thickening agent and it becomes very slimy if you use too much.

Organic cornstarch: This is a fine thickening agent for sauces. It, too, is another product you only need a small amount of, so use sparingly to prevent the taste from becoming too mealy.

MYLK

MYLK

~~~~~~~~~

I started making my own plant-based milk (mylk) a few years ago. I blogged about it and shared recipes for the pulp you end up with afterward. At the time, I preferred using a slow juicer for making my mylk instead of the cheesecloth method, because every time I used cheesecloth, the kitchen would be covered in mylk. I have long since returned to using a bowl, a strainer that fits nicely into it—that is the key—and a piece of cheesecloth.

One of the most popular drinks these days is an oat milk cappuccino, and I would have loved to come up with a homemade version for you. I experimented endlessly with ways to make the oat milk less slimy, including using amalyse powder—for that is the big problem when it comes to making oat milk at home. But nothing worked. So, I am afraid that for the best oat milk foam, you will have to go to the store and buy oat milk there, which you can then blend with a handful of soaked cashews. The addition of the cashews produces an exceptional result: much better than with store-bought oat milk alone. And unfortunately, it is a result you can never achieve with homemade oat milk. You *can* make good mylk foam at home using pure Soy Mylk (see page 17) or Almond Mylk (see page 22), similarly blended with a handful of soaked cashews for even better results.

SOY MYLK

Soybeans are an ideal basis for your vegan milk, yogurt, hangop (strained yogurt), and ice cream. Fortunately, organic soybeans are now grown in many parts of the world, making them a more sustainable choice as well.

~~~~~~~~~~~

Makes about 3 cups (700 mL / 23.6 ounces) / Keeps 3–4 days
Prep time: 12 hours to soak the soybeans / 15 minutes to make the mylk

Ingredients: ½ cup + 1 teaspoon (100 grams / 3.53 ounces) soybeans, soaked for 12 hours in about 2 cups (500 mL / 16.91 ounces) water with a pinch of ground sea salt, then rinsed — 4⅛ cups (1 L / 33.81 ounces) water for the mylk — pinch of ground sea salt — **optional flavorings:** maple syrup, vanilla extract, cinnamon, dates

Equipment: Food processor or blender — cheesecloth — strainer — large pot

~~~~~~~~~~~

1. Combine the presoaked soybeans with the 4⅛ cups water and the salt in a food processor or blender and mix until smooth. Place a piece of double-folded cheesecloth in a strainer and put the strainer over a large pot. Strain the mixture through the cheesecloth and squeeze out any excess moisture.
2. Heat the soy mylk over low heat and bring it to a rapid simmer, stirring frequently. Monitor closely. Turn it down or remove from the heat if the mylk begins to foam. If a skin forms on top, you can remove it. After 10 minutes, turn off the heat and allow the soy mylk to cool.
3. If you plan to use the soy mylk for making the Soy Yogurt (see page 74), cool it to 110°F (43°C).
4. If you are not using the mylk for the yogurt recipe, you can now flavor it as desired by adding maple syrup, vanilla extract, cinnamon, and/or dates.
5. Pour the mylk into a sterilized jar or bottle and store in the refrigerator.

PEANUT MYLK

~~~~~~~~~~~

Makes about 3 cups (700 mL / 23.6 ounces) / Keeps 3–4 days
Prep time: 8 hours to soak the peanuts / 10 minutes to make the mylk

Ingredients: 1½ cups (200 grams / 7.05 ounces) peanuts, unroasted and unsalted, soaked for 8 hours in about 2 cups (500 mL / 16.91 ounces) water with a pinch of ground sea salt, then rinsed — 3⅓ cups (800 mL / 27.05 ounces) water for the mylk — pinch of ground sea salt — **optional flavorings:** maple syrup, vanilla extract, cinnamon, dates

Equipment: Food processor or blender — cheesecloth — strainer — large bowl

~~~~~~~~~~~

1. Combine the presoaked peanuts with the 3⅓ cups water and the salt in a food processor or blender and mix until smooth. Place a piece of cheesecloth in a strainer over a bowl and strain the mixture through the cheesecloth. Squeeze out any excess moisture.
2. Add any desired flavorings such as maple syrup, vanilla extract, cinnamon, and/or dates.
3. Pour the mylk into a sterilized jar or bottle and store in the refrigerator.

Did you know that peanut mylk can also be easily made in a slow juicer? You need to presoak the peanuts, but you do not have to blend them. Scoop them into the slow juicer along with the water and salt.

Leftover pulp suggestion: Very useful as a flour substitute in sweet baking recipes.

BLACK SESAME MYLK

~~~~~~~~~~

Makes about 3 cups (700 mL / 23.6 ounces) / Keeps 3–4 days
Prep time: 1 hour to soak the sesame seeds / 10 minutes to make the mylk

Ingredients: 1¼ cups + 1 tablespoon (175 grams / 6.17 ounces) sesame seeds, soaked for 1 hour in about 2 cups (500 mL / 16.91 ounces) warm water, then rinsed — 3⅓ cups (800 mL / 27.05 ounces) water for the mylk — 4 small dates — pinch of ground sea salt — **optional flavorings:** maple syrup, vanilla extract, cinnamon

Equipment: Food processor or blender — cheesecloth — strainer — large bowl

~~~~~~~~~~

1. Mix the sesame seeds with the 3⅓ cups water, dates, and salt in a food processor or blender and mix until smooth. Place a piece of cheesecloth in a strainer over a bowl and strain the mixture through the cheesecloth. Squeeze out any excess moisture.
2. Add any desired flavorings such as maple syrup, vanilla extract, and/or cinnamon.
3. Pour the mylk into a sterilized bottle and store in the refrigerator.

NUT MYLK: ALMOND, CASHEW, OR HAZELNUT

~~~~~~~~~~

Makes about 3 cups (700 mL / 23.67 ounces) almond/hazelnut mylk or
about 4 cups (1 L / 33.81 ounces) cashew mylk / Keeps 3-4 days
Prep time: 8 hours to soak the nuts / 10 minutes to make the mylk

Ingredients: 1⅓-1½ cups (200 grams / 7.05 ounces) nuts, soaked for 8 hours in about 2 cups (500 mL / 16.91 ounces) water with a pinch of salt, then rinsed — 3⅓ cups (800 mL / 27.05 ounces) water for the mylk — pinch of ground sea salt — **optional flavorings:** maple syrup, vanilla extract, cinnamon, dates

Equipment: Food processor or blender — cheesecloth or nut milk bag (for the almond and hazelnut mylk) — strainer — large bowl

~~~~~~~~~~

Almond / Hazelnut Mylk

1. Combine the nuts with the 3⅓ cups water and salt in a food processor or blender and mix until smooth.
2. Place a piece of cheesecloth or a nut milk bag in a strainer over a bowl and strain the mixture through the cheesecloth. Squeeze out any excess moisture.
3. Add any desired flavorings such as maple syrup, vanilla extract, cinnamon, and/or dates.
4. Pour the mylk into a sterilized jar or bottle and store in the refrigerator for up to 3 days.

Cashew Mylk

1. Combine the nuts with the 3⅓ cups water and salt in a food processor or blender and mix until smooth.
2. Add any desired flavorings such as maple syrup, vanilla extract, cinnamon, and/or dates.
3. Pour the mylk into a sterilized jar or bottle and store in the refrigerator.

Suggestion for the leftover pulp: The leftover pulp makes an excellent substitute for flour, for example in the cheezecake crust (see page 77). If using, omit the tablespoon of water called for in the dough.

COCONUT MYLK

Makes about 2¾ cups (650 mL / 21.98 ounces) / Keeps 3–4 days
Prep time: 10 minutes

Ingredients: ⅞ cup (100 grams / 3.53 ounces) unsalted coconut flakes or grated coconut — 3¼ cups (750 mL / 25.36 ounces) water — pinch of ground sea salt — **optional flavorings:** maple syrup, vanilla extract, cinnamon, dates

Equipment: Food processor or blender — cheesecloth or nut milk bag — strainer — large bowl

1. Combine the coconut with the water and salt in a food processor or blender and mix until smooth. Place a piece of cheesecloth in a strainer over a bowl and strain the mixture through the cheesecloth. Squeeze out any excess moisture. Taste the mylk and strain again as needed.
2. Add any desired flavorings such as maple syrup, vanilla extract, cinnamon, and/or dates.
3. Pour the mylk into a sterilized bottle and store in the refrigerator.

Suggestion for the leftover pulp: Mix the leftover pulp with yogurt, oats, nuts, and fruit for a delicious breakfast.

RICE MYLK

~~~~~~~~~

Makes about 3 cups (700 mL / 23.67 ounces) / Keeps 3–4 days
Prep time: 10 minutes

Ingredients: 1 cup (200 grams / 7.05 ounces) cooked white or brown rice — 3⅓ cups (800 mL / 27.05 ounces) water for the mylk — pinch of ground sea salt — **optional flavorings:** maple syrup, vanilla extract, cinnamon, dates

Equipment: Food processor or blender — cheesecloth — strainer — large bowl

~~~~~~~~~

1. Combine the rice with the water and salt in a food processor or blender and mix until smooth. Place a piece of cheesecloth in a strainer over a bowl and strain the mixture through the cheesecloth. Squeeze out any excess moisture.
2. Add any desired flavorings such as maple syrup, vanilla extract, cinnamon, and/or dates.
3. Pour the mylk into a sterilized jar bottle and store in the refrigerator.

Suggestion for the leftover pulp: You should not have much pulp left over but any remaining pulp can be used in the Chai Rice Pudding recipe found on page 95.

OAT MYLK

~~~~~~~~~~

Makes about 1⅔ cups (400 mL / 13.53 ounces) / Keeps 3–4 days
Prep time: 10 minutes

Ingredients: 2¾ cups + 1 tablespoon (250 grams / 8.82 ounces) rolled oats — 4⅛ cups (1 L / 33.81 ounces) ice cold water — pinch of ground sea salt — **optional flavorings:** maple syrup, vanilla extract, cinnamon

Equipment: Blender — nut milk bag — strainer

~~~~~~~~~~

1. Combine the oats, water, and salt in a blender and blend for 10 to 30 seconds until smooth, depending on how strong your blender is. Be careful not to over blend, otherwise the mylk will become slimy. Start with 10 seconds and continue to blend 5 seconds at a time as needed.
2. Place a nut milk bag in a strainer over a bowl and pour the oat mixture very slowly into the strainer until all of the liquid has naturally run through the bag. Do not squeeze the bag or push down the oats—again, to prevent the mylk from becoming slimy.
3. Add any desired flavorings such as maple syrup, vanilla extract, and/or cinnamon.
4. Pour the mylk into a sterilized jar or bottle and store in the refrigerator.

Suggestion for the leftover pulp: Use the pulp you have left over for some of your oatmeal breakfast the next day.

Tips for preventing your mylk from becoming slimy:
- *Be sure to use ice cold water, possibly even replacing some with ice cubes.*
- *Use a fine-meshed nut milk bag or a clean fine-knit T-shirt for straining the mixture. Cheesecloth is too coarse and allows too many oats through.*
- *Soak the oats ahead of time for 15 minutes in water with two vegan capsules containing enzymes, including amylase; then rinse the oats and proceed with the recipe.*

COCONUT DULCE DE LECHE

This South American caramel makes a perfect sauce over ice cream or as a cake topping, but if you have a big sweet tooth like I do, you will surely also just sometimes want to spoon it right out of the can.

~~~~~~~~~

Makes 1 can (usually 320 grams / 11.29 ounces) / Keeps for a few weeks
Prep time: 5 minutes / Cooking time: 3–4 hours

Ingredients: 1 can sweetened condensed coconut milk

Equipment: Large pot with a lid

~~~~~~~~~

1. Fill a large pot with water and place the can of coconut milk in it. Make sure the can is covered by at least 1 inch (2 centimeters) of water. Bring the water to a boil, then simmer over low heat for 3 to 4 hours. Roll the can around every now and then and add water as needed to keep it sufficiently covered.
2. Remove the can from the water and allow it to cool completely. Shake the can well and open it. Stir the dulce de leche thoroughly and store it in a sterilized jar in the refrigerator.

FRENCH TOAST

~~~~~~~~~~

Makes 2 servings
Prep time: 20 minutes

Ingredients: 3 tablespoons chickpea flour — 2 tablespoons powdered sugar —
1 teaspoon cinnamon — 1 tablespoon nutritional yeast — ½ teaspoon kala namak or salt —
1 cup + 2 teaspoons (250 mL / 8.45 ounces) Almond Mylk (see page 22) or other plant-based
milk — ½ teaspoon vanilla extract — 1 tablespoon All-Purpose Butter (see page 39) or store-
bought plant-based butter — 6 thin or 3 thick slices stale bread, preferably sourdough

Toppings: Maple syrup — blueberries — powdered sugar —Aquafaba or
Coconut Whipped Cream (see page 73) — sliced almonds

Equipment: Mixing bowl — frying pan

~~~~~~~~~~

1. Combine the chickpea flour, powdered sugar, cinnamon, nutritional yeast, and kala namak
    or salt in a mixing bowl. Slowly add the mylk to the mixture, stirring constantly until the
    batter is smooth. Add in the vanilla extract.
2. In a frying pan, heat the butter over medium heat. Dip a slice of bread in the batter and
    cook on both sides until golden brown. Repeat with the rest of bread.
3. Garnish the French toast with the toppings as desired and serve immediately.

BUTTER

〜〜〜〜〜〜〜

BUTTER

~~~~~~~~~

In this chapter, I share recipes for several sorts of plant-based butters. If you plan to use these butters for baking and cooking, pay attention to the kind of oil you use and what its smoke point is.

ALL-PURPOSE BUTTER

~~~~~~~~~~

Makes over 1 cup (250 grams / 8.82 ounces) / Keeps 1–2 weeks
Prep time: 10 minutes

Ingredients: ⅔ cup (150 grams / 5.29 ounces) coconut oil, melted and brought to room temperature — 2 tablespoons + 1 teaspoon (35 mL / 1.18 ounces) Almond Mylk (see page 22) or other plant-based milk, at room temperature — ⅓ cup + 2 teaspoons (75 grams / 2.65 ounces) neutral oil, such as organic cold-pressed canola oil — 1 teaspoon nutritional yeast — ½ teaspoon apple cider vinegar — pinch of ground turmeric — ¼ teaspoon ground sea salt or more according to taste

Equipment: Food processor or blender — 2-cup (500 mL) storage container (approx. 4 x 6 inches / 11 x 15 centimeters) — parchment paper

~~~~~~~~~~

1. Combine all the ingredients in a food processor or blender and blend until smooth. Scrape down the sides of the bowl or jar occasionally and add salt according to taste.
2. Spoon the mixture into a storage container lined with parchment paper and refrigerate for at least 3 hours or freeze for 1 hour to harden.

You can also make this recipe with avocado oil. The butter will have a somewhat more greenish tint.

Did you know that you can also use this butter for making cookies, cakes, and buttercream?

THE SOFTIE—
SPREADABLE BUTTER

~~~~~~~~

Makes about ¾ cup (180 grams / 6.35 ounces) / Keeps 1–2 weeks
Prep time: 20 minutes

Ingredients: ⅓ cup (80 grams / 2.82 ounces) coconut oil, melted and brought to room temperature — ⅓ cup (40 grams / 1.41 ounces) cashews — 3 tablespoons + 1 teaspoon (50 mL / 1.69 ounces) water at room temperature — 2 tablespoons + 1 teaspoon (30 grams / 1.06 ounces) neutral oil, such as grapeseed oil — 1 teaspoon nutritional yeast — ½ teaspoon apple cider vinegar — pinch of turmeric — ⅓ cup (30 grams / 1.06 ounces) almond flour — ½ teaspoon sea salt or more according to taste

Equipment: Small food processor or food chopper — 2-cup (500 mL) storage container (approx. 4 x 6 inches / 11 x 15 centimeters)

~~~~~~~~

1. Combine all the ingredients except salt in a food processor or food chopper and mix until smooth. Scrape down the sides of the bowl or jar occasionally and add salt according to taste.
2. Spoon the mixture into a storage container and refrigerate for at least 3 hours to harden.

GARLIC HERB BUTTER

~~~~~~~~~

Makes about 1 cup (220 grams / 7.76 ounces) / Keeps 1–2 weeks
Prep time: 10 minutes

Ingredients: 1 cup (215 grams / 7.58 ounces) Spreadable Butter (see page 40), at room temperature — 1 clove garlic, crushed — ¼ cup (15 grams / 0.53 ounces) parsley, finely chopped — ¼ cup (15 grams / 0.53 ounces) chives, finely chopped — 2 teaspoons lemon juice — 1 teaspoon ground sea salt — ½ teaspoon Dijon mustard

~~~~~~~~~

Combine all the ingredients in a small bowl and mash with a fork until evenly distributed. Add pepper and additional salt according to taste. Allow the butter to harden in the refrigerator for at least 1 hour.

Instead of parsley and chives, you can also use your own favorite fresh herbs to create a butter entirely to your liking.

DUTCH BUTTER CAKE

~~~~~~~~

Makes 12 servings / Keeps for a few days in the refrigerator
Prep time: 10 minutes + 1 hour in the refrigerator + 30–40 minutes baking time

Ingredients: 1 cup + 1 tablespoon + 2 teaspoons (50 grams / 8.82 ounces) hard plant-based butter (store-bought or see page 39) at room temperature — ¼ cup + 2 tablespoons + 1 teaspoon (80 grams / 2.82 ounces) granulated sugar — ¼ cup + 2 tablespoons + 1 teaspoon (80 grams / 2.82 ounces) superfine sugar — 1 teaspoon vanilla extract — 1 tablespoon lemon juice — ½ teaspoon lemon zest — pinch of ground sea salt — 2⅛ cups (250 grams / 8.82 ounces) flour — 2 tablespoons plant-based milk of your choosing — 1 tablespoon maple syrup

Equipment: Stand mixer — parchment paper — 8-inch (20–22 cm) cake pan (not springform)

~~~~~~~~

1. Combine all the ingredients except the plant-based milk and maple syrup in a bowl. Mix by hand or in a stand mixer using the dough hook until dough comes together. Roll the dough out on a piece of parchment paper to the diameter of the cake pan and place in the refrigerator for 1 hour.
2. Preheat oven to 350°F (175°C).
3. Place the dough on the parchment paper in the cake pan and smooth the surface out with a spoon or small pastry roller. Mix the plant-based milk and maple syrup together in a small bowl. Brush milk mixture onto the dough. If you used store-bought butter, you can apply a checkered pattern at this point using a fork (with homemade butter, this step occurs after baking).
4. Bake the butter cake for 35 to 40 minutes until golden brown. The cake may not look done, but that is not a problem. Remove the butter cake from the oven, and if you used homemade butter, you can apply the checkered pattern now. After about 10 minutes, push the edges of the cake down so that it has the same thickness throughout. Allow the butter cake to cool in the pan for 4 to 6 hours.

* Using the All-Purpose Butter recipe on page 39? Add all the ingredients for the butter, omitting the turmeric and salt, to the ingredients in the bowl. You do not have to refrigerate the butter for 3 hours for it to harden.

DRINKS

DRINKS

~~~~~~~~

Many milk-based drinks can also easily be "veganized." You can use mylk or plant-based yogurt to make delicious hot chocolate in the winter or a refreshing mango lassi or iced coffee in the summer.

ICED COFFEE WITH VANILLA, ROSE LEAVES & CARDAMOM

~~~~~~~~~

Makes 2 servings
Prep time: Syrup: 10 minutes + 30 minutes steeping / Coffee: 10 minutes

Ingredients: **Rose cardamom syrup:** ¼ cup (60 mL / 2.03 ounces) maple syrup — ¼ cup (60 mL / 2.03 ounces) water — 2 teaspoons dried rose leaves — 4 cardamom pods, bruised — ½ teaspoon vanilla extract

Iced coffee: Ice cubes — 4 shots espresso — ¾ cup (175 mL / 5.92 ounces) Almond Mylk (see page 22)

Equipment: Small saucepan

~~~~~~~~~

Rose Cardamom Syrup

1. Mix the maple syrup with the water in a small saucepan. Bring to a boil over low heat and stir for about 2 minutes until the syrup is completely dissolved.
2. Remove the pan from the heat and add in the rose leaves, cardamom pods, and vanilla extract.
3. Allow the syrup to steep for 30 minutes, then strain into a jar or bottle.

Iced Coffee

1. Fill two glasses with ice cubes.
2. Mix the espresso with 4 tablespoons rose cardamom syrup and divide between each glass.
3. Add the mylk at the end.

You can also use crushed ice for this recipe. Place the ice cubes in a dish towel, wrap tightly, and slam against the wall.

SOY BUTTERMYLK

~~~~~~~~~~

Makes 4 servings / Keeps 2–3 days
Prep time: 15 minutes

Ingredients: 4 tablespoons lemon juice — 3½ cups (800 mL / 27.05 ounces) Soy Mylk (see page 17)

~~~~~~~~~~

1. Stir the lemon juice into the mylk and let it sit for 15 minutes.
2. Pour the mylk into a sterilized jar or bottle and store in the refrigerator. Shake before use.

BANANA–STRAWBERRY MYLK SHAKE

~~~~~~~~~~

Makes 2 servings
Prep time: 10 minutes

Ingredients: ½ cup (130 grams / 4.59 ounces) strawberries — 1 banana — 4 scoops vanilla ice cream (see page 96 and omit the cocoa and nuts) — $\frac{5}{8}$ cup (150 mL / 5.07) plant-based milk of your choosing — ¼ teaspoon vanilla extract

Equipment: Food processor or blender

~~~~~~~~~~

Combine all the ingredients in a food processor or blender and mix until smooth.

CHOCOLATE SMOOTHIE BOWL
WITH PEANUT BUTTER CARAMEL

~~~~~~~~

Makes 2 servings
Prep time: 15 minutes

Ingredients: **Peanut butter caramel sauce:** 6 tablespoons (100 grams / 3.53 ounces) peanut butter — 4 tablespoons maple syrup — ¼ teaspoon vanilla extract — ¼ teaspoon ground sea salt — 6 tablespoons water

Smoothie bowl: 1⅔ cups + 2 teaspoons (400 mL / 13.53 ounces) Soy Yogurt (see page 74) — 2 frozen bananas, peeled and cut in pieces — 3 tablespoons cocoa powder or more according to taste — **optional:** 1–2 teaspoons maple syrup

Toppings: 1 banana, sliced — mixed nuts, such as hazelnuts, walnuts, pecans — coarsely chopped chocolate — coconut flakes

Equipment: Small saucepan — food processor or blender

~~~~~~~~

Peanut Butter Caramel Sauce

1. Heat the peanut butter in a small saucepan over low heat.
2. Add the maple syrup, vanilla extract, salt, and water and stir thoroughly. Add additional water as needed to thin the sauce.
3. Set aside to cool.

Smoothie Bowl

1. Combine the yogurt, bananas, and cocoa powder in a food processor or blender and mix until smooth. Add the maple syrup if using.
2. Divide the smoothie bowl between two bowls and garnish with the toppings and the peanut butter caramel sauce. Serve immediately.

SPICY ORANGE HOT CHOCOLATE

~~~~~~~~~

Makes 2 servings
Prep time: 30 minutes

Ingredients: 2.47 ounces (70 g) semisweet chocolate — 1½ cups (350 mL / 11.83 ounces) Almond Mylk (see page 22) — 6 tablespoons + 2 teaspoons (100 mL / 3.38 ounces) orange juice (from about 2 oranges) — 1 red chili pepper with seeds, sliced into thin strips — 1 tablespoon maple syrup

Toppings: A few tablespoons Aquafaba or Coconut Whipped Cream (see page 73) — ¼ cup (20 grams / 0.71 ounces) sliced almonds, lightly roasted — pinch of chili powder

Equipment: Double boiler or small saucepan with a bowl that fits into it — strainer

~~~~~~~~~

1. Melt the chocolate in a double boiler. Once it is melted, slowly add the mylk, stirring constantly. Mix thoroughly, then add the orange juice, chili pepper, and maple syrup. Stir well, remove from the heat, and allow the mixture to steep for 10 minutes.
2. Strain the chili pepper out of the chocolate mylk. Reheat the chocolate mylk and add more mylk or maple syrup according to taste.
3. Pour the chocolate mylk into two mugs and garnish with the toppings. Serve immediately.

Prefer it a little less spicy? For a milder version, remove the seeds from the chili pepper or do not use the whole pepper.

MANGO LASSI

~~~~~~~~~~

Makes 2 servings
Prep time: 10 minutes

Ingredients: 1 ripe mango, peeled and sliced — ¾ cup (180 grams / 6.35 ounces) Soy Yogurt (see page 74) — pinch of ground sea salt — pinch of ground cardamom

Equipment: Food processor or blender

~~~~~~~~~~

1. Combine all the ingredients in a food processor or blender and mix until smooth.
2. Add more salt or cardamom according to taste. Serve immediately.

YOGURT
& CREAM

YOGURT
& CREAM

~~~~~~~~~

I use a wide range of basic ingredients for the recipes in this chapter: soy or almond milk for the yogurt, silken tofu for the quark, cashews for the crème fraiche, aquafaba for the whipped cream, and regular tofu for the cream cheeze. And the cheezecake recipe uses a mix of silken tofu, coconut milk, and chickpeas for the filling. You will discover that there are endless possibilities for creating deliciously creamy recipes in a plant-based diet.

LEMON SOY QUARK WITH COOKIE DOUGH

~~~~~~~~~

Makes 2 servings
Prep time: 4–6 hours to soak the cashews / 30 minutes to make the quark

Ingredients: **Lemon curd:** ¼ cup (30 grams / 1.06 ounces) raw cashews, soaked for
4–6 hours in about ¾ cup (200 mL / 6.76 ounces) water with a pinch of salt, then rinsed —
pinch of ground sea salt — juice of 3 organic lemons — zest of 1 organic lemon — ½ cup +
1 tablespoon (110 grams / 3.88 ounces) sugar — 1 tablespoon + 2 teaspoons
(25 mL / 0.85 ounces) water
Quark: 14.10 ounces (400 g) silken tofu — ¼ teaspoon vanilla extract —
pinch of ground sea salt
Cookie Dough: 6 dates — ⅔ cup (60 grams / 2.12 ounces) rolled oats — ⅓ cup (50 grams /
1.76 ounces) unpeeled almonds — 1 tablespoon coconut sugar — pinch of ground sea salt

Equipment: Food processor or blender — small saucepan

~~~~~~~~~

Lemon Curd

1. Combine the cashews, salt, lemon juice, lemon zest, and sugar with the water in a food processor or blender and blend until smooth.
2. Transfer the mixture to a small saucepan. Cook over medium heat for 10 minutes to thicken, stirring frequently. Set aside to cool.
3. If the mixture becomes too thick, add a bit of water and warm it up again slightly.

Quark

1. Combine the silken tofu with the vanilla extract and salt in a food processor and mix until smooth.
2. Add in one half to three fourths of the lemon curd and blend thoroughly. Set aside the rest of the lemon curd.

Cookie Dough

1. Combine the dates, oats, almonds, coconut sugar, and salt in a food processor and mix until a sticky dough forms. This takes about 5 to 10 minutes. If the dough is too sticky, add more oats.
2. Remove the dough from the processor and crumble into chunks. Store in the refrigerator until needed.

Serve the lemon quark with the remaining lemon curd and cookie dough.

CASHEW COOKING CREAM

Can be used in tomato sauce, broccoli soup, or mushroom cream sauce. You can actually use this vegan version in place of any cream in cooking.

~~~~~~~~~~

Makes 1¼–1½ cups (300–350 mL / 10.14 ounces) / Keeps 4 days
Prep time: 8 hours to soak the cashews / 10 minutes to make the cream

Ingredients: ⅞ cup (100 grams / 3.53 ounces) raw cashews, soaked for 8 hours in about 2 cups (500 mL / 16.91 ounces) water with a pinch of ground sea salt, then rinsed — ¾ cup + 1 tablespoon + 1 teaspoon (200 mL / 6.76 ounces) water — 2 teaspoons lemon juice — pinch of ground sea salt — **optional:** garlic powder, onion powder, additional lemon juice

Equipment: Small food processor, food chopper, or blender

~~~~~~~~~~

1. Combine the cashews, water, lemon juice, and salt in a food processor, food chopper, or blender and mix until smooth and creamy.
2. Add more water to reach the desired consistency and/or garlic powder, onion powder, and/or lemon juice, according to taste.
3. Store in a sterilized jar or bottle in the refrigerator.

CASHEW CRÈME FRAICHE

Makes a delicious dip for nachos or cucumber and bell pepper.

~~~~~~~~~~

Makes about ½ cup (150 grams / 5.29 ounces) / Keeps 3 days
Prep time: 8 hours to soak the cashews / 10 minutes to make the crème fraiche

Ingredients: ⁷⁄₈ cup (100 grams / 3.53 ounces) raw cashews, soaked for 8 hours in about 2 cups (500 mL / 16.91 ounces) water with a pinch of ground sea salt, then rinsed — 2 tablespoons lemon juice — 1 tablespoon water — 2 tablespoons Soy Yogurt (see page 74) — 1 clove garlic — ¼ teaspoon sea salt — ½ teaspoon dried mint — ¼ teaspoon onion powder

Equipment: Small food processor, blender, or food chopper — airtight resealable container

~~~~~~~~~~

1. Combine all the ingredients in a small food processor, blender, or food chopper and mix until smooth. Scrape down the sides of the processor, blender, or chopper with a spatula.
2. Spoon into a container and store in the refrigerator.

You can also make this recipe with soaked sunflower seeds. The crème fraiche will then have a slightly grayish tint.

CHIVE CREAM CHEEZE

~~~~~~~~~~

Makes almost 1 cup (200 grams / 7.05 ounces) / Keeps 4–5 days
Prep time: 10 minutes

Ingredients: 7.05 ounces (200 g) firm tofu — 2 tablespoons coconut oil, melted — 2 tablespoons lemon juice — ½ teaspoon fine-ground sea salt — ¼ teaspoon garlic powder — 1 tablespoon water — 3 tablespoons (10 grams / 0.35 ounces) chives, finely chopped

Equipment: Food processor or immersion blender — airtight resealable container

~~~~~~~~~~

1. Combine all the ingredients except the chives in a food processor or with an immersion blender and process until smooth.
2. Add 1 to 2 additional tablespoons of water as needed to achieve the desired consistency. Then, stir in the chives.
3. Spoon into an airtight resealable container and store in the refrigerator.

Great served on bagels, bread, or mini toasts.

AQUAFABA WHIPPED CREAM
& COCONUT WHIPPED CREAM

The aquafaba produces a stiff, yet at the same time airy, glossy whipped cream. If you prefer a thick, floppy whipped cream, try the one with coconut.

~~~~~~

Makes about 1⅔–2 cups (400–500 mL / 13.53–16.91 ounces)
Prep time: 15 minutes

Ingredients: **Aquafaba whipped cream:** 4 tablespoons aquafaba — $1/8$ teaspoon lemon juice — ½ teaspoon vanilla extract — 6–8 tablespoons powdered sugar, according to taste — 1 tablespoon mild-flavored olive oil

Coconut whipped cream: 1⅔ + 2 teaspoons (400 mL / 13.53 ounces) coconut cream or coconut milk, chilled overnight in the refrigerator — ½ teaspoon vanilla extract — 1 teaspoon maple syrup

Equipment: Hand mixer or stand mixer

~~~~~~

Aquafaba Whipped Cream

1. Combine the aquafaba, lemon juice, and vanilla extract with a hand mixer or in the bowl of a stand mixer and stir well. Set the mixer to medium speed and beat for about 5 minutes until the mixture begins to foam. Increase the speed gradually as you beat another 5 minutes until stiff peaks form.
2. Add the powdered sugar tablespoon by tablespoon, making sure each addition is fully dissolved before adding the next spoonful. Add in the oil and beat no longer than 5 seconds to prevent the cream from collapsing. Serve immediately.

Coconut Whipped Cream

1. Place a can of coconut milk or cream in the refrigerator overnight so that the water separates from the coconut and the hard part, the coconut cream, can be used to make the whipped cream.
2. Turn the can upside down and open it from the bottom. Pour out the liquid (you can use this for a smoothie) and spoon the coconut cream out of the can.
3. Mix the coconut cream with the vanilla extract and maple syrup and beat with a mixer until soft peaks form.

* This method will not work for all brands of coconut milk/cream but if you buy a can of coconut whipping cream, meant for making whipped cream, you are bound to succeed.

SOY YOGURT

You can also make this yogurt with a plant-based milk other than soy, such as almond milk or coconut milk from a can. Most yogurt starters are made specifically for soy yogurt, though, so in that case, choose a vegan yogurt as a starter.

~~~~~~~~~~~

Makes about 2 cups (500 mL / 16.91 ounces) / Keeps 3–4 days
Prep time: 12–14 hours

Ingredients: ½ teaspoon arrowroot powder — ¾ teaspoon agar-agar — 1 tablespoon water — 2 cups + 1 tablespoon + 2 teaspoons (500 mL / 16.91 ounces) Soy Mylk (see page 17) with no additives — 3 tablespoons (60 grams / 2.12 ounces) vegan yogurt with yogurt cultures or an old batch of homemade yogurt or 2 teaspoons (5 grams / 0.18 ounces) soy yogurt starter

Equipment: Saucepan — glass jar with a lid able to hold at least 2 cups (500 mL / 16.91 ounces) — kitchen thermometer — large pot with lid — ladle or spatula (sterilize all tools)

~~~~~~~~~~~

1. Mix the arrowroot and agar-agar with the water in a small bowl. Using a soy yogurt starter? Skip this step: you do not need these thickening agents.
2. Combine the mylk with the agar-agar mixture in a pan and heat over low heat to 176°F (80°C). Try to keep the mylk at 176°F (80°C) for about 10 minutes, stirring frequently.
3. Remove the pan from the heat and pour the mixture into a glass jar with a lid able to hold at least 2 cups. Let it cool to 109°F (43°C). If you are using a powdered yogurt starter, mix the powder with 2 tablespoons of water in a small bowl. Add the starter or starter yogurt to a jar and stir thoroughly. Put the lid on the jar.
4. Set the mixture aside for 8 to 12 hours, keeping it at a temperature of 104°F (40°C)–109°F (43°C). You can do this by filling a large pot with a lid with warm water (109°F [43°C]), placing the yogurt in it (ensuring that the yogurt is at least halfway covered), and wrapping the pot with the lid on it in a dish towel. You can also put the pot in a preheated oven set to 104°F (40°C). The longer the yogurt ferments, the tarter it will become. This makes a thick yogurt, which you can blend with an immersion blender if desired.
5. Store the yogurt in the refrigerator.

CHEEZECAKE WITH STRAWBERRY SAUCE

Makes 8 servings / Keeps 4 days in the refrigerator
Prep time: 2 hours + 1 night in the refrigerator

Ingredients: **Crust:** 1¼ cups (120 grams / 4.23 ounces) almond flour — 1 cup (200 grams / 7.05 ounces) sugar — 1 tablespoon water — 1 cup (90 grams / 3.17 ounces) rolled oats — ⅓ cup (80 grams / 2.82 ounces) plant-based butter at room temperature
Filling: 14.10 ounces (400 g) silken tofu — ¾ cup + 1 tablespoon + 1 teaspoon (200 mL / 6.76 ounces) coconut milk — ¾ cup + 1 tablespoon + 1 teaspoon (200 grams / 7.05 ounces) chickpeas from a can — 3 tablespoons lemon juice — 1 teaspoon lemon zest — ½ cup + 1 tablespoon + 2 teaspoons (120 grams / 4.23 ounces) sugar — 2 teaspoons vanilla extract — 1 tablespoon arrowroot powder — pinch of ground sea salt
Strawberry sauce: ½ pound (250 grams / 8.82 ounces) strawberries — 1½ tablespoons sugar — 1 tablespoon water

Equipment: Approx. 8-inch (20 cm) springform pan

~~~~~~~~~~

Cheezecake

1. Preheat oven to 350°F (180°C).
2. Mix all the ingredients for the crust in a bowl by hand and form the dough into a ball.
3. Press the dough into the bottom of a springform pan lined with parchment paper and bake for 15 minutes. Remove from the oven and let cool.
4. In a separate bowl, mix all the ingredients for the filling until smooth and pour the mixture over the crust. Tap the pan lightly on the counter to remove any air bubbles.
5. Bake in the oven for 45 to 60 minutes. Turn the oven off as soon as the outer edges of the cake are firm but the center is still a bit jiggly.
6. Leave the cheezecake in the oven with the oven turned off for 1 hour, then place it in the refrigerator overnight to set.

Strawberry Sauce

1. Place the strawberries, sugar, and water in a small saucepan. Bring to a boil over low heat for about 15 minutes. Remove the pan from the heat and allow to cool.
2. Serve the cheezecake with the strawberry sauce.

For the crust, you can also use 1½ cups (120 grams / 4.23 ounces) almond pulp instead of almond flour. In that case, add an additional ½ cup (30 grams / 1.06 ounces) rolled oats and omit the water.

DESSERTS

DESSERTS

~~~~~~~~~~

This chapter is filled with a variety of desserts: from several kinds of ice cream to my personal fave, crème brûlée; from more substantial desserts, like the chocolate mousse, to lighter ones, like the panna cotta with blueberry sauce. And the star of the chapter is agar-agar. This plant-based powder made from red algae works in the same way as gelatin, so it is fantastic for adding body to custards.

TIRAMISU

~~~~~~~~~~

Makes 4 servings
Prep time: 30 minutes / Waiting time: 1 hour

Ingredients: **Cake:** 1 cup + 2 teaspoons (125 grams / 4.41 ounces) flour — ½ cup + 2 tablespoons (125 grams / 4.41 ounces) sugar — ¼ teaspoon baking soda — pinch of salt — 6 tablespoons + 2 teaspoons (100 grams / 3.53 ounces) applesauce — 1 teaspoon vanilla extract — ½ teaspoon lemon juice — 7 tablespoons (100 grams / 3.53 ounces) plant-based butter at room temperature

Tiramisu: 14.10 ounces (400 g) silken tofu — 4 tablespoons sugar — 2 tablespoons + 1 teaspoon (35 grams / 1.23 ounces) plant-based butter at room temperature — ½ teaspoon vanilla extract — 1 tablespoon lemon juice — 2 shots espresso — 4 tablespoons Tia Maria liqueur — 2 tablespoons cocoa powder

Equipment: Cake pan — parchment paper — food processor — 6 x 8 inches (15 x 20 centimeters) — tiramisu pan

~~~~~~~~~~

1. Preheat the oven to 300°F (150°C).
2. For the cake, combine the flour, sugar, baking soda, and salt in a bowl. In a separate bowl, stir the vanilla extract and lemon juice into the applesauce. Add the liquid mixture to the dry ingredients and cut the butter in with a fork until completely absorbed. Pour the batter into a cake pan lined with parchment paper and bake for 40 minutes. Remove from the oven and let cool.
3. For the tiramisu, combine the silken tofu, sugar, butter, vanilla extract, and lemon juice in a food processor and puree until you have a smooth, silky tofu cream.
4. Cut the cake lengthwise into two layers. Mix together the espresso and the Tia Maria and quickly dunk each cake half into the mixture. Pour some of the espresso and Tia Maria mixture into the bottom of the tiramisu pan and save half for pouring over the cake. Place one layer of cake in the bottom of the tiramisu pan and pour some espresso and Tia Maria over it, then spread about half of the silky tofu cream over that cake layer. Repeat with the second layer. Smooth the top layer with a spoon and sieve the cocoa powder over it. Place the tiramisu in the refrigerator for a few hours to set.
5. If desired, sieve more cocoa over the tiramisu before serving.

Don't have time to make the cake yourself? You can also use vegan cake or ladyfingers from the store.

COCONUT CRÈME BRÛLÉE

**I think this is my favorite recipe in this book: a crunchy caramel layer covering
a silky crème still slightly warm from the kiss of the blowtorch. It's to die for.**

~~~~~~~~~

*Makes 4 servings of almost ½ cup (100 mL / 3.38 ounces) each /
Keeps 3–4 days in the refrigerator
Prep time: 8 hours to soak the cashews / 20 minutes + at least 3 hours to set*

Ingredients: ⅓ cup (40 grams / 1.41 ounces) raw cashews, soaked for 8 hours in about
¾ cup (200 mL / 6.76 ounces) water with a pinch of salt, then rinsed — 1⅔ + 2 teaspoons
(400 mL / 13.53 ounces) coconut milk — 1 tablespoon + 1 teaspoon arrowroot powder —
¾ teaspoon agar-agar — ¼ cup (70 grams / 2.47 ounces) maple syrup — 1 teaspoon vanilla
extract — pinch of ground turmeric — pinch of ground sea salt —
4 tablespoons turbinado sugar

Equipment: Food processor or blender — small saucepan — 4 crème brûlée ramekins —
crème brûlée blowtorch

~~~~~~~~~

1. Combine all the ingredients except the turbinado sugar in a food processor or blender and
   mix until smooth. Pour the mixture into a small saucepan and bring to a boil over low heat,
   stirring constantly. Slowly boil for at least 2 minutes, while continuing to stir.
2. Distribute the mixture over four ramekins and allow to cool slightly before placing in the
   refrigerator for at least 3 hours to set.
3. Shortly before serving, sprinkle the turbinado sugar over the crème brûlée and burn it with
   a blowtorch or place it under the broiler in the oven until the sugar is melted. Serve
   immediately.

SOY HANGOP (STRAINED YOGURT) WITH ORANGE SAUCE

~~~~~~~~~

Makes 2 servings / Keeps 3–4 days in the refrigerator
Prep time: 20 minutes + 8 hours

Ingredients: **Hangop:** 2 cups (500 mL / 16.91 ounces) Soy Yogurt (see page 74)
Orange sauce: 1 cup + 2 teaspoons (250 mL / 8.45 ounces) orange juice and blood orange juice —
1 small orange, cut into pieces — 3 tablespoons sugar — 1½ teaspoons organic cornstarch —
1 tablespoon water

Equipment: Dish towel, cheesecloth, or nut milk bag — strainer —
blender or immersion blender — small saucepan

~~~~~~~~~

Hangop

1. Place a dish towel, cheesecloth, or nut milk bag in a strainer over a bowl and pour the yogurt into the strainer.
2. Allow the yogurt to drain through the strainer for at least 8 hours or overnight in the refrigerator. Blend the hangop to a smooth consistency with a blender or an immersion blender as needed.

Orange Sauce

1. Heat the orange juice, orange pieces, and sugar in a small saucepan.
2. In a small bowl, mix the cornstarch and water together. Whisk the cornstarch mixture into the orange sauce. Bring to a boil over low heat and slowly boil for 15 minutes.
3. Remove the pan from the heat and allow to cool.

Serve the hangop with the orange sauce.

ALMOND-VANILLA PUDDING

~~~~~~~~

Makes about 2 cups (500 mL / 16.91 ounces) / Keeps 2–3 days in the refrigerator
Prep time: 15 minutes

Ingredients: 1 vanilla bean or 1 teaspoon vanilla extract — 2 cups + 1 tablespoon + 2 teaspoons (500 mL / 16.91 ounces) Almond Mylk (see page 22) — 2 tablespoons organic cornstarch — pinch of ground turmeric — 2 tablespoons sugar or maple syrup — pinch of ground sea salt

Equipment: Small saucepan — whisk — immersion blender

~~~~~~~~

1. Cut the vanilla bean in half lengthwise and scrape out the paste.
2. Mix the mylk with the cornstarch and turmeric in a small bowl until a smooth paste forms. Place the rest of the mylk in a small saucepan with the sugar, vanilla (bean + paste), salt, and cornstarch mixture, and heat on low, stirring with a whisk, until the mixture slowly thickens. Stir constantly to prevent clumping.
3. It is important to heat the mixture slowly without allowing it to boil. Remove the pudding from the burner as soon as it has thickened. Allow to cool, then remove the vanilla bean. Use a whisk or an immersion blender to remove any clumps.

For chocolate pudding, replace the vanilla with 3 tablespoons cocoa powder.

COCONUT-CARAMEL ICE CREAM SANDWICHES WITH CHOCOLATE & PISTACHIOS

~~~~~~~~

Makes 10 ice cream sandwiches / Keeps for 1 week
Prep time: 1 hour / Waiting time for wafers: 12 hours / Freezing time: 3 hours with an ice cream
maker or 11 hours without an ice cream maker

Ingredients: **Cookies (20):** 1¾ cups + 1 tablespoon + 1 teaspoon (220 grams / 7.76 ounces) all-purpose flour — 2 cups + 2 tablespoons + 2 teaspoons (200 grams / 7.05 ounces) oat flour — ½ cup + 1 tablespoon + 2 teaspoons (120 grams / 4.23 ounces) sugar — 2 teaspoons baking powder — ⅓ cup (50 grams / 1.76 ounces) hazelnuts, lightly roasted and coarsely chopped — ½ teaspoon ground sea salt — ¾ cup + 1 tablespoon + 1 teaspoon (200 mL / 6.76 ounces) Almond Mylk (see page 22) — 1 teaspoon vanilla extract
Salted caramel: ⅝ cup (150 mL / 5.07) coconut milk — ⅓ cup + 2 tablespoons (70 grams / 2.47 ounces) coconut sugar — 1 teaspoon ground sea salt — juice of ¼ lemon
Ice cream: 2¾ cups (650 mL / 21.98 ounces) coconut milk (2 cans for the recipe) at room temperature — ½ cup + 1 tablespoon (115 grams / 4.06 ounces) sugar — 1½ teaspoons vanilla extract — ½ teaspoon ground sea salt
Ice cream sandwiches: 7.5 ounces (200 g) semisweet chocolate — 2 tablespoons olive oil — ¾ cup (100 grams / 3.53 ounces) pistachios, lightly roasted and coarsely chopped

Equipment: 2-inch (5 centimeter) cookie cutter — small saucepan — ice cream maker or immersion blender — airtight resealable container — small ice cream scoop

~~~~~~~~

Cookies

1. Combine the all-purpose flour, oat flour, sugar, baking powder, hazelnuts, and salt in a bowl. In a separate small bowl, mix together the mylk and vanilla extract. Add this to the dry ingredients and mix with your hands until the dough is soft.
2. Roll the dough into a ball and place it in the refrigerator for 8 to 24 hours.

3. Roll out dough from ⅛ to ¼-inch (5-mm) thickness on a work surface dusted with flour. Use a 2-inch (5 centimeter) cookie cutter to cut out 20 cookies. Place the cookies on a baking sheet lined with parchment paper.

(Recipe continues on the next page.)

4. Preheat the oven to 350°F (180°C). Bake the cookies for 14 to 16 minutes in the center of the oven until golden brown. Allow cookies to cool completely.

Salted Caramel

1. Combine the coconut milk, coconut sugar, and salt in a small saucepan. Place over low heat and allow the mixture to cook down for 5 to 10 minutes, stirring regularly.
2. Remove pan from the heat, add in the lemon juice, and allow mixture to cool.

Ice Cream

1. Combine half the coconut milk with the sugar, vanilla extract, and salt in a pan and heat until the sugar is dissolved. Remove the pan from the heat, add in the rest of the coconut milk, and set aside to cool.
2. Once cool, place the mixture in the refrigerator until the temperature reaches 50°F (10°C).

Ice Cream Maker Method
Prepare the ice cream according to the manufacturer instructions. Stir the caramel through the ice cream at the end. Scoop the ice cream into an airtight resealable container and place it in the freezer for at least 2 hours.

Method without an Ice Cream Maker
Pour the coconut milk mixture into an airtight resealable container and place it in the freezer. After half an hour, stir the ice cream thoroughly with an immersion blender, using a fork for the edges. Repeat this every half hour for 3 hours (set an alarm each time!) until the ice cream is creamy, then stir in the caramel and allow the ice cream to harden in the freezer for another 7 to 8 hours.

Ice Cream Sandwiches

1. Portion out 10 scoops of ice cream using a small ice cream scoop, placing each one between two cookies. Press together to form an ice cream sandwich. Place back in the freezer for at least 1 hour.
2. Melt the chocolate in a double boiler and add in the olive oil.
3. Dip the ice cream sandwiches in the melted chocolate and sprinkle with pistachio nuts.

Make chocolate ice cream by adding ½ cup plus 1½ tablespoons (50 grams) cocoa powder. The cocoa makes the mixture so smooth and creamy that there is no need to stir it while it is freezing.

CHAI RICE PUDDING

~~~~~~~~~

Makes about 2 cups (500 mL / 16.91 ounces) / Keeps 2 days in the refrigerator
Prep time: 40 minutes

Ingredients: **Rice pudding:** ½ cup (100 grams / 3.53 ounces) arborio rice — 3 cups (700 mL / 23.67 ounces) Rice Mylk (see page 26) or other plant-based milk of your choosing — 3 tablespoons maple syrup — pinch of ground sea salt — ½ teaspoon vanilla extract
Chai sauce: 4 tablespoons plant-based milk of your choosing — 4 tablespoons powdered sugar — 1 teaspoon cinnamon — ½ teaspoon ground cardamom — ½ teaspoon ginger powder — ½ teaspoon ground cloves
Topping: Handful of pecans

Equipment: Small saucepan — glasses/mason jars

~~~~~~~~~

Rice Pudding

1. Combine all the ingredients for the pudding in a small saucepan and bring to a boil.
2. Slowly simmer over low heat for about 30 minutes, stirring occasionally, until the risotto is soft and the pudding has thickened.

Chai Sauce

1. Combine all the ingredients for the sauce in a small saucepan and heat until the mixture is smooth. Allow it to thicken slightly for a few minutes, then remove pan from the heat and set aside to cool. The sauce will continue to thicken a bit more.
2. Add more mylk as needed to make the sauce thinner or extra powdered sugar to make it thicker until desired consistency is reached.

Serve the rice pudding with chai sauce and top with pecans.

CASHEW-VANILLA-CHOCOLATE ICE CREAM WITH WALNUTS & HAZELNUTS

~~~~~~~~~~

Makes about 2 cups (500 mL / 16.91 ounces) /
Keeps for a few weeks but tastes best within 1 week
Prep time: 8 hours to soak the cashews / 20 minutes to make the ice cream /
Freezing time: 2 hours with an ice cream maker or 11 hours without an ice cream maker

Ingredients: 1 cup + 2 teaspoons (250 mL / 8.45 ounces) Almond Mylk (see page 22) — ¼ cup + 2 tablespoons + 1 teaspoon (80 grams / 2.82 ounces) granulated sugar — 1¾ cups (200 grams / 7.05 ounces) raw cashews, soaked for 8 hours in about 2 cups (500 mL / 16.91 ounces) water with a pinch of ground sea salt, then rinsed — 1½ tablespoons (20 grams / 0.71 ounces) coconut oil, melted — 1 teaspoon vanilla extract — ½ teaspoon ground sea salt — ⅔ cup + 1 tablespoon (60 grams / 2.12 ounces) cocoa powder — ½ cup (70 grams / 2.47 ounces) hazelnuts and walnuts, lightly roasted and coarsely chopped

Equipment: Small saucepan — food processor or blender — ice cream maker or immersion blender — airtight resealable container

~~~~~~~~~~

1. Stir the mylk and sugar in a pan until the sugar dissolves.
2. Puree the cashews in a food processor or blender until smooth. This can take 10 to 20 minutes.
3. Add the almond mylk mixture, coconut oil, vanilla extract, salt, and cocoa powder to the cashew puree and mix another 1 to 2 minutes. Place in the refrigerator until the temperature of the mixture reaches 50°F (10°C).

Ice Cream Maker Method

Prepare the ice cream according to manufacturer instructions. Stir the nuts through the ice cream at the end. Scoop the ice cream into a container and place it in the freezer for at least 2 hours.

Method without an Ice Cream Maker

Pour the cashew mixture into a container and place it in the freezer. After half an hour, stir the ice cream thoroughly with an immersion blender, using a fork for the edges. Repeat this every half hour for 3 hours (set an alarm each time!), then stir in the nuts. Allow the ice cream to harden in the freezer another 7 to 8 hours.

Make vanilla ice cream by leaving out the cocoa powder, hazelnuts, and walnuts. Vanilla ice cream made this way is delicious in mylk shakes (see page 52).

CHOCOLATE MOUSSE WITH
CARAMELIZED ALMOND SLICES & SEA SALT

~~~~~~~~~~~

Makes an ample 6 servings / Keeps 2 days in the refrigerator
Prep time: 8 hours to soak the cashews / 30 minutes to make the mousse

Ingredients: **Chocolate mousse:** 1 cup + 2 teaspoons (250 mL / 8.45 ounces) Almond Mylk (see page 22) — ⅓ cup + 1 tablespoon (60 grams / 2.12 ounces) coconut sugar — 1¾ cups (200 grams / 7.05 ounces) raw cashews, soaked for 8 hours in about 4 cups (1 L / 33.81 ounces) water with a pinch of ground sea salt, then rinsed — 1½ tablespoons (20 grams / 0.71 ounces) coconut oil, melted and brought to room temperature — ½ cup (40 grams / 1.41 ounces) cocoa powder — 1 teaspoon vanilla extract — ½ teaspoon ground sea salt
Caramelized almond slices: ¼ cup (20 grams / 0.71 ounces) sliced almonds, lightly roasted — 2 tablespoons sugar — 1 tablespoon mild olive oil — 1 teaspoon coarse sea salt (Maldon)

Equipment: Food processor or blender — small saucepan — parchment paper

~~~~~~~~~~~

Chocolate Mousse

1. Heat the mylk and sugar in a pan over low heat. Stir thoroughly until sugar dissolves.
2. Puree the cashews in a food processor or blender until smooth. This can take 10 to 20 minutes.
3. Add the almond mylk mixture, coconut oil, cocoa powder, vanilla extract, and salt to the cashew puree and puree for another 1 to 2 minutes. Place in the refrigerator.

Caramelized Almond Slices

1. Heat a small saucepan on medium-high. Add in the sliced almonds, sugar, and olive oil and cook until the almonds are golden brown.
2. Dump the caramelized almonds out onto a sheet of parchment paper, separate them, and allow to cool thoroughly.

Garnish the chocolate mousse with caramelized almond slices and sea salt.

ROSE & BERRY FROZEN YOGURT

~~~~~~~~~

Makes about 2 cups (500 mL / 16.91 ounces) /
Keeps for a few weeks but tastes best within 1 week
Prep time: 40 minutes / Waiting time: 30 minutes / Freezing time: 2 hours with an ice cream
maker or 11 hours without an ice cream maker

Ingredients: **Blackberry sauce:** ⅓ pint (125 grams / 4.41 ounces) blackberries —
1 tablespoon coconut sugar — 2 tablespoons water — 1 teaspoon rose water
Frozen yogurt: 2 cups (500 mL / 16.91 ounces) Soy Yogurt (see page 74) or other plant-based
yogurt — ½ cup + 1 tablespoon (115 grams / 4.06 ounces) sugar — 1 teaspoon vanilla extract —
½ teaspoon ground sea salt

Equipment: Small saucepan — airtight resealable container — ice cream maker or
immersion blender

~~~~~~~~~

Blackberry Sauce

1. Combine the blackberries with the coconut sugar and water in a small saucepan. Bring to a boil, then cook for 10 minutes on low heat.
2. Remove the pan from the heat, stir in the rose water, and set aside to cool.

Ice Cream

1. Mix the yogurt, sugar, vanilla extract, and salt in a bowl.
1. Place the bowl in the refrigerator until the temperature of the mixture reaches 50°F (10°C).

Ice Cream Maker Method

Prepare the frozen yogurt according to the manufacturer instructions. Scoop it into an airtight resealable container and distribute the blackberry sauce on top in large globs. Using the backside of a spoon, swirl the sauce through the frozen yogurt. Place in the freezer for at least 2 hours.

Method without an Ice Cream Maker

Pour the yogurt mixture into an airtight resealable container and place it in the freezer. After half an hour, stir the frozen yogurt thoroughly with an immersion blender, using a fork for the edges. Repeat this every half hour for 3 hours (set an alarm each time!). Then, distribute the blackberry sauce on top of the ice cream in large globs. Use the backside of a spoon to create lovely swirls. Allow the frozen yogurt to harden in the freezer for another 7 to 8 hours.

COCONUT PANNA COTTA
WITH BLUEBERRY SAUCE

~~~~~~~~~~

Makes 6 servings / Keeps 2 days in the refrigerator
Prep time: 25 minutes + a few hours in the refrigerator

Ingredients: **Panna cotta:** 1⅔ cups + 2 teaspoons (400 mL / 13.53 ounces) coconut milk
— 1⅔ cups + 2 teaspoons (400 mL / 13.53 ounces) Almond Mylk (see page 22) — 3 tablespoons
sugar — zest of 1 lime and 4 teaspoons lime juice — 1 teaspoon vanilla extract — ¾ teaspoon
agar-agar — pinch of ground sea salt
Blueberry sauce: ⅓ pint (125 grams / 4.41 ounces) blueberries — 2 tablespoons water —
1 tablespoon coconut sugar — ½ teaspoon cinnamon

Equipment: Pudding molds — small saucepan — whisk

~~~~~~~~~~

Panna Cotta

1. Grease the pudding molds lightly with oil.
2. Combine the coconut milk, almond mylk, sugar, lime zest and juice, vanilla extract, agar-agar, and salt in a small saucepan and bring to a boil over low heat, stirring with a whisk. Allow the mixture to slowly boil for at least 2 minutes, stirring frequently. Pour the mixture into the molds and allow to cool, then refrigerate for several hours so that it sets.
3. After 10 minutes, stir the panna cotta in the refrigerator thoroughly to prevent the coconut milk from separating.

Blueberry Sauce

1. Place the berries, water, coconut sugar, and cinnamon in a small saucepan.
2. Bring to a boil, then for about 15 minutes on low heat. Remove the pan from the heat and allow to cool.

Allow the panna cotta to set for several hours in the refrigerator and serve with the blueberry sauce.

CHEEZE

CHEEZE

As I mentioned in the preface to this book, it helps to remain open-cheeze-minded when it comes to trying or making vegan cheese. See it as a new kind of cheese, one that exists alongside the more traditional kinds. You will find that you quickly become accustomed to all the new flavors vegan cheeze has to offer.

The cheezes in this chapter are all fairly simple. They can be made relatively quickly and do not need to ripen for weeks at a time. Only the goat cheeze needs to ripen for two days unrefrigerated. You can also easily adapt the recipes according to your own taste once you learn how to work with the ingredients, for example by adding more nutritional yeast for a cheezier flavor, more white miso for added umami, or more lemon juice to make the cheeze a bit crisper and sharper.

CUMIN CHEEZE

This cheeze is best served on thin slices on bread.

~~~~~~~~~~

Makes 1 (15.87 ounces / 450 g) block of cheeze / Keeps for 1 week
Prep time: 30 minutes + a few hours' hardening time

Ingredients: 6½ tablespoons (75 grams / 2.65 ounces) cooked white or brown rice —
1 tablespoon (8 grams / 0.28 ounces) nutritional yeast — 2 teaspoons lemon juice —
¼ teaspoon garlic powder — 1 tablespoon + 1 teaspoon white miso — pinch of ground
turmeric — 1 teaspoon sea salt — 1⅔ cups + 2 teaspoons (400 mL / 13.53 ounces) Rice Mylk
(see page 26) or other plant-based milk — ¼ cup (60 mL / 2.03 ounces) organic canola oil or
other neutral oil that can be heated — 2 tablespoons agar-agar — 1 tablespoon cumin seeds

Equipment: Food processor — small saucepan — whisk — cheese mold (e.g., silicon or
ceramic mold measuring 4 x 4 inch [10 x 10 centimeter])

~~~~~~~~~~

1. Combine the rice, nutritional yeast, lemon juice, garlic powder, miso, turmeric, salt, and a
   little bit of the mylk in a food processor. Blend until smooth, scraping down the sides every
   now and then.
2. Heat the remaining mylk and the oil in a small saucepan. Add the agar-agar, while whisking
   constantly. Bring the mixture to a boil and let it cook for at least 2 minutes.
3. Remove the pan from the heat. Add the mylk mixture to the rice mixture and blend until
   everything is well combined.
4. Grease a cheese mold with a bit of oil. Pour the mixture into the mold and stir in the cumin
   seeds. Allow to cool and place into the refrigerator for several hours to harden.

GOAT CHEEZE

~~~~~~~~~~

Makes 6.17 ounces (175 g) / Keeps 5–7 days
Prep time: 8 hours to soak the nuts / 15 minutes to make the cheeze + 2 days fermentation

Ingredients: ⅞ cup (100 grams / 3.53 ounces) raw cashews + ¼ cup (40 grams / 1.41 ounces) macadamia nuts, soaked for 8 hours in about 4 cups (1 L / 33.81 ounces) water with a pinch of ground sea salt, then rinsed — ¼ teaspoon ground sea salt — pinch of black pepper — 1 tablespoon water — 2 tablespoons probiotic yogurt — 2 teaspoons lemon juice — 2 vegan probiotic capsules

Equipment: Small food processor or blender — cheesecloth — strainer or cheese mold with holes — bowl

~~~~~~~~~~

1. Combine all the ingredients except the probiotic capsules in a small food processor or blender and mix until you have a shaggy mass. You can also blend until smoother if you want a softer, more spreadable version. Scrape down the sides of the bowl or jar with a spatula.
2. If the mixture has warmed up in the processor or blender, allow it to cool. Then, add the contents of the probiotic capsules and mix briefly.
3. Place some cheesecloth in a strainer or cheese mold with holes set over a bowl and spoon the mixture into the cheesecloth. Fold the cheesecloth bundle closed.
4. Place the bowl with the cheeze mixture in a warm spot for 2 to 3 days, such as an oven that is turned off. Check it every now and then and place in the refrigerator once the goat cheeze has a suitably sharp flavor.

PARMEZAN CHEEZE

~~~~~~~~~

Makes 4.23 ounces (120 g) / Keeps for 1 week
Prep time: 15 minutes

Ingredients: 1 teaspoon white wine vinegar — ½ teaspoon lemon juice — ¼ teaspoon Dijon mustard — ½ teaspoon onion powder — ½ teaspoon garlic powder — ⅓ cup (40 grams / 1.41 ounces) cashews, lightly roasted — 3 tablespoons (30 grams / 1.06 ounces) macadamia nuts, lightly roasted — 3½ tablespoons (30 grams / 1.06 ounces) pine nuts, lightly roasted — 3 tablespoons nutritional yeast — ¼ teaspoon ground sea salt

Equipment: Small food processor or food chopper

~~~~~~~~~

1. Mix together the white wine vinegar, lemon juice, mustard, onion powder, and garlic powder.
2. Combine the mixture in a small food processor or food chopper with the remaining ingredients and blend until you have a shaggy mass that is slightly sticky. Add more salt according to taste. Mold the parmezan cheeze in whatever shape you want in a piece of parchment paper and store in the freezer.

Prefer a grated version for sprinkling? Mix 3 tablespoons nutritional yeast with some garlic powder, onion powder, and ground sea salt for a quick grated cheeze.

NOZZARELLA FOR GRILLED CHEEZE AND PIZZA

~~~~~~~~~

Makes 1 large ball nozzarella / Keeps 3–4 days
Prep time: 30 minutes

Ingredients: 2 tablespoons psyllium husk flakes — ⅓ cup + 2 teaspoons (90 mL / 30.04 ounces) water — 8.82 ounces (250 g) firm tofu — 4 tablespoons tapioca flour — 1 tablespoon apple cider vinegar — 1 tablespoon nutritional yeast — 1 cup + 1 tablespoon + 2 teaspoons (265 mL / 8.96 ounces) water — 1½ teaspoons salt — 1 teaspoon garlic powder — ¼ teaspoon onion powder — 1 teaspoon maple syrup — ¼ cup (60 mL / 2.03 ounces) mild olive oil

Equipment: Food processor or blender — small saucepan

~~~~~~~~~

1. Mix the psyllium husk flakes with the water in a small bowl. Let sit for a few minutes.
2. Then, combine all the ingredients in a food processor or blender and mix until smooth.
3. Pour the mixture into a small saucepan and cook over low heat while stirring with a spatula. Stir constantly until the mixture comes completely together, about 5 to 10 minutes. Be sure to scrape the sides and bottom of the pan so that the cheeze does not burn. Remove the pan from the heat and spoon the mass into a round bowl. Allow to cool, then store in the refrigerator.

Grilled cheeze suggestion: pesto and sun-dried tomatoes.

TRIO OF MINI FRENCH CASHEW CHEEZES: APRICOT & THYME, PAPRIKA & PEPPER, AND ROSE & PISTACHIO

〰〰〰〰〰〰

Makes 3 small cheeze disks / Keeps 4–5 days
Prep time: 8 hours to soak the cashews / 20 minutes + 1 night to make the cheezes

Ingredients: 1¼ cups (140 grams / 4.94 ounces) raw cashews, soaked for 8 hours in about 3¼ cups (750 mL / 25.36 ounces) water with a pinch of salt, then rinsed — 2 tablespoons nutritional yeast — ½ tablespoon white miso — 1 tablespoon lemon juice — 1 small clove garlic — 4 tablespoons water — 1 tablespoon coconut oil, melted and brought to room temperature — ½ teaspoon ground sea salt

Apricot & thyme: 2 dried apricots, finely chopped — 3 tablespoons (10 grams / 0.35 ounces) fresh thyme, leaves stripped

Paprika & pepper: ¼ teaspoon smoked paprika — 2 teaspoons mixed peppercorns

Roses & pistachio: 2 teaspoons rose leaves — 1–2 tablespoons (10 grams / 0.35 ounces) pistachios, finely chopped

Equipment: Food processor or blender — cheesecloth — strainer — bowl — silicon molds

〰〰〰〰〰〰

1. Combine the cashews, nutritional yeast, miso, lemon juice, garlic, and water in a food processor or blender and mix until smooth.
2. Place a piece of cheesecloth in a strainer over a bowl and spoon the mixture into the cheesecloth. Fold the cheesecloth closed and place the mixture in the refrigerator overnight.
3. Divide the mixture into 3 equal portions. Mix the apricots through one portion and the smoked paprika powder through another, then scoop each into a silicon mold and allow to harden in the refrigerator for several hours.
4. Remove the cheezes from the molds. Cover the apricot cheeze with thyme, the paprika cheeze with peppercorns, and the third cheeze with rose leaves and pistachios.

SOY PANEER

~~~~~~~~~~

Makes 5.29 ounces (150 g) / Keeps 2 days
Prep time: 15 minutes + 8 hours

Ingredients: 4$\frac{1}{8}$ cups + 1 tablespoon + 1 teaspoon (1 L / 33.81 ounces) Soy Mylk (see page 17) — ¼ cup + 2 teaspoons (70 mL / 2.37 ounces) lemon juice — pinch of ground sea salt

Equipment: Small saucepan — cheesecloth — strainer — bowl

~~~~~~~~~~

1. Mix the mylk with the lemon juice in a small saucepan and bring to a boil. Cook down for about 10 to 15 minutes over low heat, stirring regularly.

2. Place some cheesecloth in a strainer over a bowl and pour the mixture into the strainer. Allow the paneer to drain and squeeze out the cheesecloth. Do not squeeze out all of the moisture, though, to prevent the paneer from falling apart later. Add salt according to taste. Flatten out the paneer and knead into the desired shape. Wrap the paneer back in the cheesecloth and place it between two plates. Refrigerate for at least 8 hours.

This paneer is nice and crumbly, so make sure to use a good sharp knife when cutting it into cubes.

TOFETA IN OIL

~~~~~~~~~

Makes just over 10.58 ounces (300 g) / Keeps for 1 week in the refrigerator
Prep time: 30 minutes

Ingredients: 8.82 ounces (250 g) firm tofu — 1 teaspoon white miso — 1 teaspoon nutritional yeast — 4 tablespoons water — 4 tablespoons coconut oil — 1 tablespoon lemon juice — 1 teaspoon sea salt — ¼ teaspoon onion powder — ¼ teaspoon garlic powder — 1 tablespoon agar-agar — 2 teaspoons olive oil — fresh herbs (2 sprigs oregano, 3 sprigs thyme, 1 sprig rosemary) — 1 dried red pepper, halved lengthwise— 2 cups (500 mL / 16.91 ounces) extra virgin olive oil — **optional:** roasted seeds, such as cumin or coriander seeds

Equipment: Food processor or blender — small saucepan — airtight sealable container — large glass jar with lid

~~~~~~~~~

1. Combine the tofu, miso, nutritional yeast, water, coconut oil, lemon juice, salt, onion powder, garlic powder, agar-agar, and the 2 teaspoons olive oil in a food processor or blender and mix until smooth.
2. Spoon the mixture into a small saucepan over medium-high heat, stirring frequently. Cook for at least 2 minutes and remove from the heat. Spoon the mixture into an airtight resealable container and cool slightly, then place in the refrigerator for several hours.
3. Cut the tofeta into cubes and place these in a large glass jar with a lid. Add the herbs, red pepper, and extra virgin olive oil. Marinate for 2 days in the refrigerator. You can also add some roasted seeds, such as cumin or coriander seeds.

For a quick version, cut a block of tofu into cubes and put them in a glass jar with the herbs, pepper, and oil. Marinate for 2 days in the refrigerator.

CHEEZE FONDUE

~~~~~~~~~~

For 2 people
Prep time: 1 hour to soak the cashews / 30 minutes to make the fondue

Ingredients: ¼ pound (120 grams / 4.23 ounces) potatoes, peeled — 1⅓ cups (150 grams / 5.29 ounces) raw cashews, soaked for 1 hour in about 3¼ cups (750 mL / 25.36 ounces) water with a pinch of salt, then rinsed — 2 tablespoons nutritional yeast — 1 tablespoon + 2 teaspoons lemon juice — 1 tablespoon + 2 teaspoons apple cider vinegar — 2 cloves garlic — 1 tablespoon white miso — 2 tablespoons tapioca flour — 1¼ cups (300 mL / 10.14 ounces) + 4 tablespoons water, divided — 1 teaspoon ground sea salt — 1 teaspoon psyllium husk flakes — 1 cup + 2 teaspoons (250 mL / 8.45 ounces) white wine

Equipment: Food processor or blender — small saucepan

~~~~~~~~~~

1. Bring a pot of amply salted water to a boil and cook the potatoes in it until soft, about 12 to 15 minutes. Combine the cooked potatoes with the cashews, nutritional yeast, lemon juice, apple cider vinegar, garlic, miso, tapioca flour, 1¼ cups water, and salt in a food processor or blender and mix until smooth.
2. Mix the psyllium husk flakes with 4 tablespoons water in a small bowl and allow it to thicken, then add this to the potato mixture and mix for another 1 to 2 minutes.
3. Pour the mixture into a small saucepan and heat on medium-high, stirring frequently. Add in the white wine and stir thoroughly until the mixture thickens.
4. Add more miso, salt, or pepper according to taste and pour the cheeze fondue into a fondue pan. Serve immediately.

Delicious served with pieces of sourdough bread, cauliflower florets, bell pepper, carrots, tomatoes, and asparagus.

EGGS & SAUCES

EGGS & SAUCES

~~~~~~~~

Chickpeas play a prominent role in this chapter. The scrambled "eggs," for example, are made eggy by the addition of chickpea flour (and kala namak, of course), the mayonnaise gets its fluffiness from aquafaba, or chickpea liquid, and the vegan meringue would not be a vegan meringue without that same starchy chickpea liquid.

The easiest way to get some aquafaba is from a can of chickpeas (although it is now also sold as a stand-alone product). You can use the drained chickpeas for the Cheezecake recipe in this book (see page 77) or in such dishes as hummus or roasted chickpeas with spices for snacking. Fortunately, aquafaba can also be frozen for later use. Put it in an ice cube tray so you have easy access to small amounts whenever you need some.

TOAST WITH SCRAMBLED TOFU

~~~~~~~~~~

Makes 2 servings
Prep time: 20 minutes

Ingredients: ½ cup (40 grams / 1.41 ounces) chickpea flour — 2 tablespoons nutritional yeast — 1 teaspoon kala namak or salt — 1 clove garlic, minced — 1 onion, diced — pinch of ground turmeric — pinch of pepper — 2 teaspoons Dijon mustard — ⅓ cup (80 mL / 2.71 ounces) water — 7.05 ounces (200 g) tofu, crumbled — 1 tablespoon olive oil — a few slices of toasted bread — 2 tablespoons (5 grams / 0.18 ounces) chives, finely chopped

Equipment: Frying pan

~~~~~~~~~~

1. Combine the chickpea flour, nutritional yeast, kala namak or salt, garlic, onion, turmeric, and pepper in a bowl. Add in the mustard, water, and tofu and mix well.
2. Heat the olive oil in a frying pan on medium and fry the tofu mixture for 8 to 10 minutes.

Serve the scrambled tofu on bread and garnish with chives.

AQUAFABA MERINGUE WITH COFFEE-RASPBERRY SWIRL

~~~~~~~~~~

Makes 8 meringues / Keeps for 1 week
Prep time: 15 minutes + 4 hours

Ingredients: **Coffee syrup:** ¼ cup (50 grams / 1.76 ounces) sugar — 1 shot espresso
Raspberry sauce: ⅓ pint (125 grams /4.41 ounces) raspberries — 1 tablespoon sugar —
3 tablespoons water
Meringue: ½ cup (120 mL / 4.06 ounces) aquafaba — ¼ teaspoon cream of tartar — 1 teaspoon
vanilla extract — pinch of sea salt — 2 cups (225 grams / 7.94 ounces) powdered sugar

Equipment: Small saucepan — strainer — hand mixer or stand mixer

~~~~~~~~~~

Coffee Syrup

Dissolve the sugar in the espresso in a small saucepan over low heat and set aside to cool.

Raspberry Sauce

Cook the raspberries, sugar, and water in a small saucepan over low heat until the sugar is dissolved and the raspberries break down. Run the mixture through a strainer and allow to cool.

Meringue

1. Preheat the oven to 212°F (100°C) and line a baking sheet with parchment paper.
2. Combine the aquafaba, cream of tartar, vanilla extract, and salt with a hand mixer or in the bowl of a stand mixer fitted with the whisk attachment. Mix at medium-high speed until stiff peaks form. Gradually add in the sugar,

allowing each tablespoon to be stirred several times until fully dissolved.
3. Scoop the meringue onto the baking sheet and divide into two portions. Spoon the coffee syrup carefully through one and the raspberry sauce carefully through the other. Then, use a spatula to shape the meringue into individual dollops measuring 5–7 centimeters in diameter.
4. Bake the meringues in the oven for 2 hours. Do not open the oven door during that time. After 2 hours, turn the oven off and let the meringues cool in the oven for at least 2 hours, until you can remove them from the parchment paper without difficulty.

Save the leftover raspberry pulp to stir through your yogurt for breakfast.

AQUAFABA MAYONNAISE

~~~~~~~~~

Makes over ¾ cup (200 mL / 6.76 ounces) / Keeps 5 days
Prep time: 15 minutes

Ingredients: 3 tablespoons aquafaba — 1 tablespoon apple cider vinegar — 2 teaspoons maple syrup — 1 teaspoon Dijon mustard — ¼ teaspoon kala namak or salt according to taste — pinch of turmeric — ¾ cup + 1 tablespoon + 1 teaspoon (200 mL / 6.76 ounces) grapeseed oil or other neutral oil

Equipment: Deep bowl — blender or immersion blender — airtight sealable container

~~~~~~~~~

1. Combine all ingredients except the oil in a deep bowl and puree with a blender or an immersion blender. Once the mixture is foamy, add the oil in a very thin stream. It is important to do this slowly so that the mayonnaise continues to thicken. Mix for at least 5 to 10 minutes.
2. Store the mayonnaise in a container in the refrigerator.

   For mustardy mayonnaise: Add 2 tablespoons of mustard.
   For garlicky mayonnaise: Add 2 small cloves or 1 large clove minced garlic.

Use the chickpeas left over from draining off the aquafaba in a salad or for the filling in the Cheezecake recipe (see page 77).

TZATZIKI

~~~~~~~~~~

Makes 1 serving / Keeps 2 days
Prep time: 1 hour and 10 minutes

Ingredients: 1 clove garlic, minced, or more according to taste — 1 tablespoon olive oil — ½ cucumber, peeled, deseeded, and grated — pinch of ground sea salt — ¾ cup (180 grams / 6.35 ounces) Soy Yogurt (see page 74) — 3 tablespoons (10 grams / 0.35 ounces) dill, finely chopped — 1 tablespoon lemon juice

Equipment: Strainer

~~~~~~~~~~

1. Combine the garlic with the oil in a small bowl and set aside.
2. Place the cucumber in a strainer, sprinkle with salt, and allow to sweat for 1 hour.
3. Combine the drained cucumber with the yogurt, dill, and lemon juice, then add the garlic-infused olive oil. Add salt and pepper to taste.

ROASTED GARLIC SAUCE

This sauce works great as a mushroom cream sauce with risotto or a pasta sauce with grilled vegetables.

~~~~~~~~~~

Makes about 3 cups (700 mL / 23.6 ounces) / Keeps 5 days in the refrigerator
Prep time: 8 hours to soak the cashews / 10 minutes to make the sauce + 30 minutes in the oven

Ingredients: 1 bulb garlic — 1 tablespoon olive oil — 1¾ cups (200 grams / 7.05 ounces) raw cashews, soaked for 8 hours in about 4 cups (1 L / 33.81 ounces) water with a pinch of sea salt, then rinsed —1¼ cups (300 mL / 10.14 ounces) plant-based milk of your choosing — 2 tablespoons lemon juice — 1 tablespoon nutritional yeast — ¼ teaspoon onion powder — 1 teaspoon white miso — 1 teaspoon cayenne pepper — 6 tablespoons + 2 teaspoons (100 mL / 3.38 ounces) water — pinch of ground sea salt

Equipment: Baking dish — food processor or blender

~~~~~~~~~~

1. Preheat the oven to 392°F (200°C).
2. Cut the top of the garlic bulb off so that you can see the cloves. Place the bulb in a baking dish and sprinkle with the olive oil and salt and pepper. Bake in the oven for about 30 minutes until the garlic is lightly browned. Press the cloves of garlic out into a small bowl and mix with the olive oil from the baking dish.
3. Combine the garlic-infused olive-oil with the cashews, plant-based milk, lemon juice, nutritional yeast, onion powder, white miso, cayenne pepper, water, and salt in a food processor or blender and mix until smooth. Add more water as needed to achieve the desired thickness.

BÉCHAMEL SAUCE

This béchamel sauce is perfect for a vegan lasagna.

~~~~~~~~~~

Makes enough for 1 lasagna / Keeps 2 days in the refrigerator
Prep time: 20 minutes

Ingredients: 1⅔ cups + 2 teaspoons (400 mL / 13.53 ounces) Almond Mylk (see page 22)
— 2 shallots, diced — 1 bay leaf — 1 teaspoon sea salt — ½ teaspoon pepper — 3 tablespoons
(40 grams / 1.41 ounces) All Purpose Butter (see page 39) — ¼ cup (30 grams / 1.06 ounces)
flour — pinch of ground sea salt — pinch of pepper — pinch of ground nutmeg —
pinch of cayenne pepper

Equipment: Small saucepan — strainer — whisk

~~~~~~~~~~

1. Combine the mylk with the shallots, bay leaf, salt, and pepper in a small saucepan and
   bring to a boil over low heat. Slowly boil for 5 to 10 minutes. Strain the shallots and the bay
   leaf out of the mylk and set it aside.
2. Heat the saucepan on medium-high and melt the butter. As soon as it is melted, gradually
   whisk in the flour.
3. Add in the mylk and spices and stir well. Cook briefly until the desired thickness is
   achieved. If the sauce becomes too thick too quickly, dilute it with a little bit of water.

*Use the béchamel sauce immediately or store it in the refrigerator and reheat it later,
adding a little bit of water if needed.*

THANK YOU!

You don't make a cookbook all by yourself, and many people helped make this book a reality. I could not have done it without all of you.

~~~~~~~~~

Thanks to the Dutch publisher, Uitgeverij Becht, for originally putting out this book. *Lorain Grabowski, Mara Joustra, Marieke Dijkman, Anne ter Hark, Nicolette Garritsen,* and *Agatha Oudhuis*: without you this book would not be here. It was, once again, a great collaboration, and I was so glad you could be so patient and flexible. *Esther Snel,* tremendous thanks for the gorgeous design.

Pap and Mam, thank you for so extensively tasting my recipes and for your advice and support. From the time I was little, you have always supported my choices, and you have been my biggest fans from the very beginning. Thank you for your love, always. I dedicate this book to you with a full heart.

Mon bébé, my foundation and refuge! The days of playing Tetris with an overloaded fridge are over. It was an intense project, one that demanded a lot of you too: not just patience, but also a lot of space in our small apartment. Thank you for all your love and support, no matter the circumstances. You are my very dearest. My other very dearest and bit of sunshine: *Lou*. We are so blessed to have such a little gourmet as you. I enjoy your love and energy endlessly. You create nice, relaxing moments in the midst of busy times and show me what really matters.

Thank you, *family, friends*, and *neighbors* for your support, enthusiasm, endless tasting, and brainstorming and to *my best girlfriends* for constantly motivating and encouraging me and for your joyful energy.

Inge Pouw, from The Secret Props Room, you offered me the use of your props for making this book. A few weeks later, I showed up at your warehouse with my photography equipment and the first dishes and we got to work. No effort was spared. Need another wall color or backdrop painted? No problem. Let's do it! Nothing was too much. Doing the photography at your place gave me the freedom to be creative. I am infinitely grateful—for your beautiful props, your assistance with the styling, your delicious soups, your wonderful care—for everything! I think you can provide a tremendous service to many other people as well with all those beautiful props—such a wide assortment, too—at The Secret Props Room: @thesecretpropsroom. *Noa van Beek*, you were at so unbelievably many of the shoot days; every time I turned around, you had handled some detail or other within the blink of an eye. On top of that, you were a spectacular hand model!

Bibi van Beurden, Nerissa Haak, and Sam van Vlijmen, thank you so much for your help during the shoots.

The Bird Tsang, thank you for the use of your gorgeous dishware.

My forever sister-in-law, Lotte van Dam, what a joy to do the photography and styling together with you. It was a very special day with an equally beautiful result to show for it!

Thank you Siegalit Zarr and Wende Stroet, for the extra babysitting for Lou, all your good care, tasting the dishes, and of course, the mylk frother.

I am also extremely grateful for my enthusiastic recipe testers: Tom Squires, Beau Broekhof, Dinesha and Max van der Pol, Floor Heijerman, Evelijn Hekker, and Alisa Summerfield.

Thank you as well to: Daniël Krijnen and Viola Puhalovic for reading the drafts and Gonzalo Lercari for your critical eye as we put the finishing touches on the photography; Thomas Tukker, who was always ready to answer my technical questions; and Sander Veeneman for the wonderful profile photo.

Suus and Johann of Food Bandits, thanks to your tips, I finally managed a number of

years ago to make a vegan meringue after multiple failed attempts.

In addition, I was lucky enough to have access to a number of specialists I could ask questions of or work things out with. I learned so much, and still have much to learn, from each and every one of them. Thank you truly to cookbook writer Joke Boon, Marieke Laméris of the Lekker Lupine platform, FerMentor Bart Smit, food photographer Jan Bartelsman, and coffee expert Jeroen Veldkamp.

And to everyone who contributed in any way, shape, or form to the making of this book: thank you very much!

THANK YOU!

141

INDEX

~~~~~~~~~

Originally published under the title *50 x Vegan zuivel* by Uitgeverij J.H. Gottmer/H.J.W. Becht bv, Haarlem, The Netherlands; a division of Gottmer Uitgeversgroep BV

Text and recipes Marleen Visser
Recipe photographs Marleen Visser
Author's photographs Sander Veeneman | Milk Maid Project (p. 7)
Styling & food styling Marleen Visser
Props The Secret Props Room (except pp. 32, 64, 67, 76, 82, and 119: The Bird Tsang)
Backdrops The Secret Props Room
Cover and interior design Esther Snel
English translation Nina Woodson

Skyhorse Publishing books may be purchased in bulk at special discounts for sales promotion, corporate gifts, fund-raising, or educational purposes. Special editions can also be created to specifications. For details, contact the Special Sales Department, Skyhorse Publishing, 307 West 36th Street, 11th Floor, New York, NY 10018 or info@skyhorsepublishing.com.

Skyhorse® and Skyhorse Publishing® are registered trademarks of Skyhorse Publishing, Inc.®, a Delaware corporation.

Visit our website at www.skyhorsepublishing.com.

10 9 8 7 6 5 4 3 2 1

Library of Congress Cataloging-in-Publication Data is available on file.

Print ISBN: 978-1-5107-7763-7
Ebook ISBN: 978-1-5107-7764-4

Printed in China